50 Japanese Premium Cooking Recipes for Home

By: Kelly Johnson

Table of Contents

- Ramen
- Sushi (Nigiri and Maki)
- Sashimi
- Takoyaki
- Okonomiyaki
- Tempura
- Donburi (Rice Bowl)
- Chirashi-zushi
- Tonkatsu
- Unagi (Grilled Eel)
- Sukiyaki
- Shabu-shabu
- Miso Soup
- Onigiri (Rice Balls)
- Gyoza (Dumplings)
- Katsu Curry
- Nasu Dengaku (Miso Glazed Eggplant)
- Yakiniku (Grilled Meat)
- Chawanmushi (Savory Egg Custard)
- Oden
- Udon Noodle Soup
- Soba Noodles
- Kappa Maki (Cucumber Roll)
- Yaki Imo (Grilled Sweet Potato)
- Dorayaki (Red Bean Pancakes)
- Matcha Tiramisu
- Anmitsu (Jelly Dessert)
- Wagashi (Japanese Sweets)
- Ikura Don (Salmon Roe Rice Bowl)
- Yuba (Tofu Skin)
- Karage (Fried Chicken)
- Hiyayakko (Chilled Tofu)
- Kinpira Gobo (Sautéed Burdock Root)
- Shirasu Don (Whitebait Rice Bowl)
- Tamagoyaki (Japanese Omelette)

- Nikujaga (Meat and Potato Stew)
- Zaru Soba (Chilled Soba)
- Mentaiko Pasta
- Katsu Sandwich
- Sweet Potato Soba
- Somen Noodles
- Miso-marinated Fish
- Tofu Steak
- Tsukemono (Pickled Vegetables)
- Yaki Soba (Fried Noodles)
- Chashu Pork
- Goya Champuru (Bitter Melon Stir-fry)
- Yudofu (Hot Tofu)
- Shio Ramen (Salt Ramen)
- Gyudon (Beef Bowl)

Ramen

Ingredients:

- 4 cups chicken or vegetable broth
- 2 packs instant ramen noodles (discard the seasoning packets)
- 2 soft-boiled eggs
- 1 cup cooked chicken or pork, sliced
- 1 cup bok choy or spinach
- 1 green onion, sliced
- 1 tbsp soy sauce
- 1 tbsp miso paste (optional)
- Seaweed sheets (for garnish)

Instructions:

1. **Heat Broth:** In a pot, heat broth, soy sauce, and miso paste over medium heat.
2. **Cook Noodles:** Add ramen noodles and cook according to package instructions until tender.
3. **Add Vegetables:** Stir in bok choy or spinach during the last minute of cooking.
4. **Serve:** Divide noodles and broth into bowls, top with sliced chicken, soft-boiled eggs, green onions, and seaweed.

Sushi (Nigiri and Maki)

Ingredients:

- 2 cups sushi rice
- 2 1/2 cups water
- 1/2 cup rice vinegar
- 2 tbsp sugar
- 1/2 tsp salt
- Assorted fish (e.g., tuna, salmon) for nigiri
- Nori sheets for maki
- Fillings for maki (e.g., cucumber, avocado, crab)

Instructions:

1. **Prepare Rice:** Rinse sushi rice until water runs clear. Combine rice and water in a rice cooker or pot; cook according to instructions.
2. **Season Rice:** In a small saucepan, heat rice vinegar, sugar, and salt until dissolved. Pour over cooked rice and mix gently.
3. **Make Nigiri:** Wet hands and form small balls of rice, topping each with a slice of fish.
4. **Make Maki:** Place a nori sheet on a bamboo mat, spread rice evenly, add fillings, and roll tightly. Slice into pieces.

Sashimi

Ingredients:

- Assorted sashimi-grade fish (e.g., tuna, salmon, yellowtail)
- Soy sauce (for dipping)
- Wasabi (optional)
- Pickled ginger (for serving)

Instructions:

1. **Slice Fish:** Using a sharp knife, slice the fish into thin pieces. Aim for a 1/4 inch thickness.
2. **Serve:** Arrange sashimi on a plate with soy sauce, wasabi, and pickled ginger on the side.

Takoyaki

Ingredients:

- 1 cup all-purpose flour
- 1 1/4 cups dashi (Japanese soup stock)
- 1 large egg
- 1/2 cup cooked octopus, diced
- 1/4 cup green onions, chopped
- 1/4 cup tempura scraps (tenkasu)
- Takoyaki sauce (for drizzling)
- Japanese mayo (for drizzling)
- Bonito flakes and aonori (seaweed flakes) for garnish

Instructions:

1. **Make Batter:** In a bowl, mix flour, dashi, and egg until smooth.
2. **Heat Takoyaki Pan:** Preheat a takoyaki pan over medium heat and oil the wells.
3. **Add Batter:** Pour batter into each well until full. Add octopus, green onions, and tempura scraps.
4. **Cook:** Cook for about 3-4 minutes until the bottom is golden. Flip using a skewer to cook the other side.
5. **Serve:** Drizzle with takoyaki sauce and mayo, then sprinkle with bonito flakes and aonori.

Okonomiyaki

Ingredients:

- 2 cups all-purpose flour
- 1 1/2 cups dashi or water
- 2 large eggs
- 2 cups shredded cabbage
- 1/2 cup green onions, chopped
- 1/2 cup cooked pork belly or shrimp (optional)
- Okonomiyaki sauce (for drizzling)
- Japanese mayo (for drizzling)
- Aonori (seaweed flakes) for garnish

Instructions:

1. **Make Batter:** In a bowl, mix flour, dashi, and eggs until combined.
2. **Add Vegetables:** Stir in cabbage, green onions, and pork or shrimp if using.
3. **Cook:** Heat a skillet over medium heat and pour in the batter to form a pancake. Cook for 4-5 minutes on each side until golden brown.
4. **Serve:** Drizzle with okonomiyaki sauce and mayo, then sprinkle with aonori.

Tempura

Ingredients:

- 1 cup all-purpose flour
- 1/2 cup cornstarch
- 1 cup cold water
- Assorted vegetables (e.g., sweet potatoes, bell peppers, zucchini)
- Shrimp (peeled and deveined)
- Oil for frying

Instructions:

1. **Make Batter:** In a bowl, whisk together flour, cornstarch, and cold water until just combined (lumps are fine).
2. **Heat Oil:** In a deep pot, heat oil to 350°F (175°C).
3. **Fry:** Dip vegetables and shrimp in the batter, then carefully place in the hot oil. Fry until golden, about 2-3 minutes.
4. **Drain:** Remove tempura and drain on paper towels. Serve with dipping sauce (like tentsuyu).

Donburi (Rice Bowl)

Ingredients:

- 2 cups cooked rice
- 1 lb protein (chicken, beef, or tofu), sliced
- 1 onion, sliced
- 2 cups vegetables (bell peppers, carrots)
- 1/4 cup soy sauce
- 1 tbsp mirin (optional)
- 1 tbsp sugar
- Green onions for garnish

Instructions:

1. **Cook Protein:** In a skillet, sauté protein and onions until cooked through.
2. **Add Vegetables:** Stir in vegetables and cook until tender.
3. **Make Sauce:** Add soy sauce, mirin, and sugar; simmer for a few minutes.
4. **Serve:** Spoon the mixture over cooked rice and garnish with green onions.

Chirashi-zushi

Ingredients:

- 2 cups sushi rice
- 2 1/2 cups water
- 1/2 cup rice vinegar
- 2 tbsp sugar
- 1/2 tsp salt
- Assorted toppings (sliced sashimi, avocado, cucumber, pickled ginger)

Instructions:

1. **Prepare Rice:** Rinse sushi rice until water runs clear. Combine rice and water in a rice cooker or pot; cook according to instructions.
2. **Season Rice:** In a small saucepan, heat rice vinegar, sugar, and salt until dissolved. Pour over cooked rice and mix gently.
3. **Assemble:** In a bowl, mound seasoned rice and arrange assorted toppings on top.

Enjoy creating these delicious Japanese dishes!

Tonkatsu

Ingredients:

- 1 lb pork loin or pork chops
- Salt and pepper to taste
- 1 cup all-purpose flour
- 2 large eggs, beaten
- 1 cup panko breadcrumbs
- Oil for frying
- Tonkatsu sauce (for serving)

Instructions:

1. **Prepare Pork:** Season the pork with salt and pepper.
2. **Breading Station:** Set up three bowls: one with flour, one with beaten eggs, and one with panko.
3. **Bread Pork:** Dredge each pork piece in flour, dip in egg, then coat with panko.
4. **Heat Oil:** In a skillet, heat oil over medium-high heat.
5. **Fry:** Fry the pork until golden brown and cooked through, about 5-7 minutes per side. Drain on paper towels.
6. **Serve:** Slice and serve with tonkatsu sauce.

Unagi (Grilled Eel)

Ingredients:

- 1 lb unagi (grilled eel, typically pre-cooked)
- 1/2 cup eel sauce (nitsume)
- Cooked rice (for serving)

Instructions:

1. **Prepare Eel:** If using pre-cooked unagi, heat it gently in a pan or grill until warmed through.
2. **Glaze with Sauce:** Brush eel with eel sauce and grill for a few minutes until caramelized.
3. **Serve:** Serve over a bed of rice with extra eel sauce on the side.

Sukiyaki

Ingredients:

- 1 lb thinly sliced beef
- 1 onion, sliced
- 2 cups napa cabbage, chopped
- 1 cup shiitake mushrooms, sliced
- 1 block tofu, cubed
- 1/2 cup soy sauce
- 1/4 cup mirin
- 1/4 cup sugar
- 2 cups cooked rice (for serving)

Instructions:

1. **Prepare Sauce:** In a bowl, mix soy sauce, mirin, and sugar.
2. **Cook Beef:** In a hot skillet or shallow pot, add beef and cook until browned.
3. **Add Vegetables:** Add onion, cabbage, mushrooms, and tofu.
4. **Add Sauce:** Pour sauce over everything and simmer until vegetables are tender.
5. **Serve:** Serve hot with rice.

Shabu-shabu

Ingredients:

- 1 lb thinly sliced beef or pork
- 6 cups dashi or beef broth
- Assorted vegetables (bok choy, mushrooms, carrots, tofu)
- Ponzu sauce (for dipping)
- Cooked rice or udon noodles (optional)

Instructions:

1. **Heat Broth:** In a hot pot or large pot, bring dashi or broth to a simmer.
2. **Prepare Ingredients:** Arrange sliced meat and vegetables on a platter.
3. **Cook Meat:** Dip slices of meat into the simmering broth for a few seconds until cooked.
4. **Add Vegetables:** Cook vegetables in the broth until tender.
5. **Serve:** Serve with ponzu sauce and rice or noodles, if desired.

Miso Soup

Ingredients:

- 4 cups dashi or vegetable broth
- 3 tbsp miso paste
- 1/2 cup tofu, cubed
- 1/4 cup green onions, sliced
- 1/4 cup seaweed (wakame, optional)

Instructions:

1. **Heat Broth:** In a pot, heat dashi or vegetable broth over medium heat.
2. **Dissolve Miso:** In a small bowl, mix miso paste with a little warm broth to dissolve, then stir back into the pot.
3. **Add Ingredients:** Stir in tofu, green onions, and seaweed.
4. **Serve:** Heat through and serve hot.

Onigiri (Rice Balls)

Ingredients:

- 2 cups sushi rice
- 2 1/2 cups water
- Salt to taste
- Fillings (pickled plum, tuna, or salmon)
- Nori sheets (for wrapping)

Instructions:

1. **Cook Rice:** Rinse sushi rice until water runs clear. Cook with water in a rice cooker or pot.
2. **Season Rice:** Once cooked, let it cool slightly, then sprinkle with salt.
3. **Form Balls:** Wet your hands and shape a small portion of rice around your filling, forming a triangle or ball.
4. **Wrap:** Wrap with a strip of nori if desired.

Gyoza (Dumplings)

Ingredients:

- 1 lb ground pork or chicken
- 1 cup cabbage, finely chopped
- 1/4 cup green onions, chopped
- 2 cloves garlic, minced
- 1 tbsp soy sauce
- 1 tbsp sesame oil
- Gyoza wrappers
- Oil for frying
- Soy sauce for dipping

Instructions:

1. **Make Filling:** In a bowl, combine meat, cabbage, green onions, garlic, soy sauce, and sesame oil.
2. **Fill Wrappers:** Place a spoonful of filling in the center of a gyoza wrapper. Wet the edges, fold in half, and pinch to seal.
3. **Cook Gyoza:** In a skillet, heat oil over medium heat. Add gyoza and fry until the bottom is golden.
4. **Steam:** Add a little water to the skillet, cover, and steam until cooked through.
5. **Serve:** Serve with soy sauce for dipping.

Katsu Curry

Ingredients:

- 1 lb chicken or pork cutlets
- Salt and pepper to taste
- 1 cup all-purpose flour
- 2 large eggs, beaten
- 1 cup panko breadcrumbs
- Oil for frying
- 2 cups Japanese curry sauce (store-bought or homemade)
- Cooked rice (for serving)

Instructions:

1. **Prepare Cutlets:** Season the cutlets with salt and pepper.
2. **Breading Station:** Set up three bowls: flour, beaten eggs, and panko.
3. **Bread Cutlets:** Dredge cutlets in flour, dip in egg, then coat with panko.
4. **Fry:** Heat oil in a skillet over medium-high heat. Fry cutlets until golden and cooked through, about 5-7 minutes per side.
5. **Serve:** Slice the cutlets and serve over rice with warm curry sauce poured on top.

Enjoy making and savoring these delicious Japanese dishes!

Nasu Dengaku (Miso Glazed Eggplant)

Ingredients:

- 2 medium eggplants
- 1/4 cup miso paste (white or red)
- 2 tbsp sugar
- 1 tbsp mirin
- 1 tbsp sake (optional)
- Sesame seeds (for garnish)
- Green onions (for garnish)

Instructions:

1. **Prepare Eggplants:** Cut eggplants in half lengthwise. Score the flesh in a crisscross pattern and sprinkle with salt. Let sit for 10-15 minutes, then rinse and pat dry.
2. **Make Miso Glaze:** In a bowl, mix miso paste, sugar, mirin, and sake until smooth.
3. **Grill Eggplants:** Preheat the grill or broiler. Brush the cut side of the eggplants with the miso glaze and grill for about 5-7 minutes until tender and caramelized.
4. **Garnish and Serve:** Sprinkle with sesame seeds and green onions before serving.

Yakiniku (Grilled Meat)

Ingredients:

- 1 lb beef (ribeye, sirloin, or brisket), thinly sliced
- Marinade:
    - 1/4 cup soy sauce
    - 2 tbsp sake
    - 2 tbsp mirin
    - 1 tbsp sugar
    - 2 cloves garlic, minced
    - 1 tsp grated ginger

Instructions:

1. **Marinate Meat:** Combine marinade ingredients in a bowl. Add sliced beef and let marinate for at least 30 minutes.
2. **Preheat Grill:** Heat a grill or grill pan over medium-high heat.
3. **Grill Meat:** Remove meat from marinade and grill for 1-2 minutes on each side until cooked to your liking.
4. **Serve:** Serve hot with rice and dipping sauces, if desired.

Chawanmushi (Savory Egg Custard)

Ingredients:

- 4 large eggs
- 2 cups dashi broth
- 1 tbsp soy sauce
- 1 tbsp mirin
- Fillings: shrimp, chicken, mushrooms, and green onions

Instructions:

1. **Prepare Mixture:** In a bowl, whisk together eggs, dashi, soy sauce, and mirin until smooth.
2. **Add Fillings:** Divide shrimp, chicken, mushrooms, and green onions among small cups or ramekins.
3. **Steam:** Pour egg mixture over fillings. Cover each cup with aluminum foil. Steam over simmering water for 15-20 minutes until set.
4. **Serve:** Allow to cool slightly before serving.

Oden

Ingredients:

- 4 cups dashi broth
- 1/4 cup soy sauce
- 1 tbsp mirin
- Ingredients:
    - Daikon radish, peeled and sliced
    - Boiled eggs
    - Fish cakes (ganmo, chikuwa)
    - Tofu (firm or silken)
    - Konnyaku (konjac noodles or blocks)

Instructions:

1. **Make Broth:** In a large pot, combine dashi, soy sauce, and mirin. Bring to a simmer.
2. **Add Ingredients:** Add daikon, boiled eggs, fish cakes, tofu, and konnyaku. Simmer for 30-40 minutes until everything is tender.
3. **Serve:** Serve hot with a side of mustard for dipping.

Udon Noodle Soup

Ingredients:

- 4 cups dashi or chicken broth
- 2 servings udon noodles
- 1/4 cup soy sauce
- 1 tbsp mirin
- Toppings: green onions, tempura, mushrooms, and sliced fish cakes

Instructions:

1. **Cook Noodles:** Cook udon noodles according to package instructions; drain and set aside.
2. **Prepare Broth:** In a pot, heat dashi or chicken broth, soy sauce, and mirin.
3. **Combine:** Add cooked udon noodles to the broth and simmer for a few minutes.
4. **Serve:** Ladle into bowls and top with desired toppings.

Soba Noodles

Ingredients:

- 8 oz soba noodles
- 4 cups water
- Dipping sauce (soba tsuyu):
    - 1/4 cup soy sauce
    - 1/4 cup mirin
    - 1/4 cup dashi broth
- Garnishes: sliced green onions, wasabi, and nori

Instructions:

1. **Cook Noodles:** Bring water to a boil, add soba noodles, and cook according to package instructions; drain and rinse under cold water.
2. **Make Dipping Sauce:** In a bowl, combine soy sauce, mirin, and dashi.
3. **Serve:** Serve soba noodles cold with dipping sauce on the side, garnished with green onions and wasabi.

Kappa Maki (Cucumber Roll)

Ingredients:

- 1 cup sushi rice
- 1 1/4 cups water
- 2 tbsp rice vinegar
- 1 tbsp sugar
- 1/2 tsp salt
- 1 cucumber, cut into thin strips
- Nori sheets

Instructions:

1. **Prepare Rice:** Rinse sushi rice until water runs clear. Cook with water in a rice cooker or pot.
2. **Season Rice:** In a small bowl, mix rice vinegar, sugar, and salt until dissolved. Pour over cooked rice and mix gently.
3. **Make Rolls:** Place a nori sheet on a bamboo mat, spread a thin layer of rice, and place cucumber strips in the center. Roll tightly and slice into pieces.

Yaki Imo (Grilled Sweet Potato)

Ingredients:

- 2 medium Japanese sweet potatoes (satsumaimo)

Instructions:

1. **Prep Sweet Potatoes:** Wash and scrub the sweet potatoes.
2. **Grill:** Wrap each sweet potato in aluminum foil and place on a grill or in a hot oven (around 400°F/200°C) for about 45-60 minutes, until tender.
3. **Serve:** Unwrap and serve warm as a snack or side dish.

Enjoy making and savoring these delightful Japanese dishes!

Dorayaki (Red Bean Pancakes)

Ingredients:

- **For the Pancakes:**
    - 1 cup all-purpose flour
    - 1/2 tsp baking powder
    - 2 large eggs
    - 1/3 cup sugar
    - 1/4 cup milk
    - 1 tbsp honey
- **For the Filling:**
    - 1 cup red bean paste (anko)

Instructions:

1. **Make Batter:** In a bowl, whisk eggs and sugar until light. Mix in milk and honey. Sift in flour and baking powder, and stir until smooth.
2. **Cook Pancakes:** Heat a non-stick pan over medium-low heat. Pour 1/4 cup of batter to form a pancake. Cook until bubbles form on the surface, then flip and cook until golden.
3. **Assemble:** Place a spoonful of red bean paste between two pancakes. Serve warm or at room temperature.

Matcha Tiramisu

Ingredients:

- 1 cup heavy cream
- 1/2 cup mascarpone cheese
- 1/4 cup sugar
- 1 tbsp matcha powder (plus extra for dusting)
- 1 cup strong brewed green tea, cooled
- 12 ladyfinger cookies

Instructions:

1. **Whip Cream:** In a bowl, whip heavy cream until soft peaks form. In another bowl, mix mascarpone, sugar, and matcha until smooth. Fold whipped cream into the mascarpone mixture.
2. **Layer:** Quickly dip ladyfingers in green tea and layer in a dish. Spread half of the matcha mixture over the ladyfingers. Repeat layers.
3. **Chill:** Refrigerate for at least 4 hours or overnight. Dust with matcha before serving.

Anmitsu (Jelly Dessert)

Ingredients:

- 2 cups water
- 1/2 cup agar-agar powder
- 1/4 cup sugar
- Toppings:
    - Red bean paste (anko)
    - Mochi pieces
    - Fresh fruits (such as strawberries, peaches, and melon)
    - Sweet syrup (mitsu)

Instructions:

1. **Make Jelly:** In a pot, combine water, agar-agar powder, and sugar. Bring to a boil, then simmer for about 5 minutes. Pour into a mold and let it cool until set.
2. **Cut Jelly:** Once set, cut the jelly into cubes.
3. **Assemble:** Serve jelly cubes in bowls with toppings and drizzle with sweet syrup.

Wagashi (Japanese Sweets)

Ingredients:

- **For the Sweet Dough:**
    - 1 cup mochiko (sweet rice flour)
    - 1/2 cup sugar
    - 1/2 cup water
- **Fillings (varied):**
    - Red bean paste, fruit, or matcha

Instructions:

1. **Make Dough:** In a bowl, mix mochiko, sugar, and water until smooth.
2. **Steam:** Pour the mixture into a steamer and steam for about 15 minutes until translucent.
3. **Shape:** Once cooled, divide the dough and fill with your choice of filling. Shape into balls or desired forms.

Ikura Don (Salmon Roe Rice Bowl)

Ingredients:

- 2 cups cooked rice
- 1 cup ikura (salmon roe)
- 1/4 cup sliced green onions
- 1 tbsp soy sauce
- Nori strips (for garnish)

Instructions:

1. **Prepare Rice:** Serve hot cooked rice in bowls.
2. **Top with Ikura:** Spoon ikura over the rice.
3. **Garnish:** Drizzle with soy sauce and sprinkle with green onions and nori strips.

Yuba (Tofu Skin)

Ingredients:

- 1 lb fresh yuba (tofu skin) or homemade
- Soy sauce (for dipping)
- Optional: scallions and sesame seeds for garnish

Instructions:

1. **Prepare Yuba:** If using fresh yuba, cut into strips.
2. **Serve:** Serve chilled or lightly blanched with soy sauce for dipping. Garnish with scallions and sesame seeds if desired.

Karage (Fried Chicken)

Ingredients:

- 1 lb chicken thighs, boneless and skinless
- 2 tbsp soy sauce
- 1 tbsp sake
- 1 tbsp ginger, grated
- 1 clove garlic, minced
- 1/2 cup potato starch (or cornstarch)
- Oil for frying

Instructions:

1. **Marinate Chicken:** In a bowl, combine chicken, soy sauce, sake, ginger, and garlic. Let marinate for at least 30 minutes.
2. **Coat Chicken:** Dredge marinated chicken pieces in potato starch.
3. **Fry:** Heat oil in a deep pan over medium-high heat. Fry chicken until golden brown and cooked through, about 5-7 minutes. Drain on paper towels.
4. **Serve:** Serve hot with a side of lemon and dipping sauce.

Hiyayakko (Chilled Tofu)

Ingredients:

- 1 block silken tofu
- Toppings:
    - Grated ginger
    - Green onions, sliced
    - Soy sauce
    - Bonito flakes (optional)

Instructions:

1. **Prepare Tofu:** Drain and cut the tofu into cubes.
2. **Serve:** Place tofu on a serving plate and top with grated ginger, green onions, and bonito flakes.
3. **Drizzle:** Serve with soy sauce on the side for dipping.

Enjoy making and indulging in these delightful Japanese dishes!

Kinpira Gobo (Sautéed Burdock Root)

Ingredients:

- 1 medium burdock root (gobo)
- 1 medium carrot, julienned
- 2 tbsp soy sauce
- 1 tbsp mirin
- 1 tbsp sugar
- 1 tbsp sesame oil
- 1 tbsp sesame seeds (for garnish)

Instructions:

1. **Prepare Burdock:** Peel the burdock root and slice it into thin matchsticks. Soak in water to prevent browning.
2. **Sauté:** Heat sesame oil in a pan over medium heat. Add burdock and carrot, and sauté for about 5-7 minutes until tender.
3. **Season:** Stir in soy sauce, mirin, and sugar, and cook for an additional 2-3 minutes.
4. **Serve:** Garnish with sesame seeds and serve warm or at room temperature.

Shirasu Don (Whitebait Rice Bowl)

Ingredients:

- 2 cups cooked rice
- 1 cup shirasu (whitebait)
- 1/4 cup green onions, sliced
- Soy sauce (for drizzling)
- Nori strips (for garnish)

Instructions:

1. **Prepare Rice:** Serve cooked rice in bowls.
2. **Top with Shirasu:** Distribute shirasu over the rice.
3. **Garnish:** Sprinkle with green onions and nori strips. Drizzle with soy sauce before serving.

Tamagoyaki (Japanese Omelette)

Ingredients:

- 4 large eggs
- 1 tbsp soy sauce
- 1 tbsp mirin
- 1 tsp sugar
- Oil for frying

Instructions:

1. **Prepare Mixture:** In a bowl, whisk together eggs, soy sauce, mirin, and sugar until smooth.
2. **Heat Pan:** Heat a rectangular or non-stick frying pan and lightly oil it.
3. **Cook Layers:** Pour a thin layer of egg mixture into the pan. Cook until the edges set, then roll it up to one side of the pan. Pour another layer of egg mixture and lift the rolled omelette to let the new mixture flow underneath. Repeat until all the egg is used.
4. **Slice and Serve:** Remove from the pan, let cool slightly, and slice into pieces.

Nikujaga (Meat and Potato Stew)

Ingredients:

- 1/2 lb thinly sliced beef
- 2 medium potatoes, peeled and cut into chunks
- 1 onion, sliced
- 1 carrot, sliced
- 2 cups dashi or beef broth
- 1/4 cup soy sauce
- 2 tbsp mirin
- 1 tbsp sugar

Instructions:

1. **Sauté Ingredients:** In a pot, brown the beef over medium heat. Add onion, potatoes, and carrot, and sauté for a few minutes.
2. **Add Broth and Seasonings:** Pour in dashi or broth, soy sauce, mirin, and sugar. Bring to a simmer.
3. **Cook:** Cover and simmer for about 20-30 minutes until the vegetables are tender.
4. **Serve:** Serve warm over rice.

Zaru Soba (Chilled Soba)

Ingredients:

- 8 oz soba noodles
- 1/4 cup soy sauce
- 1/4 cup mirin
- 1/4 cup dashi broth
- Toppings: sliced green onions, wasabi, nori strips

Instructions:

1. **Cook Noodles:** Boil soba noodles according to package instructions. Drain and rinse under cold water to cool.
2. **Make Dipping Sauce:** In a bowl, mix soy sauce, mirin, and dashi.
3. **Serve:** Serve cold soba noodles on a plate with dipping sauce on the side. Garnish with green onions, wasabi, and nori strips.

Mentaiko Pasta

Ingredients:

- 8 oz spaghetti
- 1/2 cup mentaiko (spicy cod roe)
- 1/4 cup heavy cream
- 2 tbsp butter
- 1 clove garlic, minced
- Chopped green onions (for garnish)
- Seaweed strips (for garnish)

Instructions:

1. **Cook Pasta:** Boil spaghetti according to package instructions.
2. **Prepare Sauce:** In a pan, melt butter over medium heat and sauté garlic until fragrant. Add mentaiko and cream, stirring until combined.
3. **Combine:** Add cooked pasta to the sauce, tossing to coat.
4. **Serve:** Garnish with green onions and seaweed strips before serving.

Katsu Sandwich

Ingredients:

- 1 lb pork loin or chicken breast, pounded thin
- Salt and pepper to taste
- 1 cup flour
- 2 large eggs, beaten
- 1 cup panko breadcrumbs
- Oil for frying
- 4 slices of soft bread (shokupan)
- Tonkatsu sauce (for serving)

Instructions:

1. **Bread Meat:** Season the meat with salt and pepper. Dredge in flour, dip in egg, and coat with panko.
2. **Fry:** Heat oil in a skillet over medium heat. Fry breaded meat until golden brown and cooked through, about 5-7 minutes per side. Drain on paper towels.
3. **Assemble Sandwich:** Cut the katsu in half and place between two slices of bread. Drizzle with tonkatsu sauce and top with the remaining bread.

Sweet Potato Soba

Ingredients:

- 8 oz soba noodles
- 1 medium sweet potato, peeled and diced
- 1 tbsp olive oil
- 1 clove garlic, minced
- 2 tbsp soy sauce
- 1 tsp sesame oil
- Chopped green onions (for garnish)

Instructions:

1. **Cook Sweet Potato:** Boil sweet potato until tender. Drain and set aside.
2. **Cook Noodles:** Boil soba noodles according to package instructions. Drain and rinse under cold water.
3. **Sauté Ingredients:** In a pan, heat olive oil and sauté garlic until fragrant. Add sweet potato, soy sauce, and sesame oil. Stir to combine.
4. **Combine:** Toss the sweet potato mixture with soba noodles. Garnish with green onions before serving.

Somen Noodles

Ingredients:

- 8 oz somen noodles
- 1/4 cup soy sauce
- 1/4 cup mirin
- 1/4 cup dashi broth
- Toppings: sliced green onions, grated ginger, shiso leaves

Instructions:

1. **Cook Noodles:** Boil somen noodles according to package instructions. Drain and rinse under cold water.
2. **Make Dipping Sauce:** In a bowl, combine soy sauce, mirin, and dashi.
3. **Serve:** Serve somen noodles cold with dipping sauce and toppings on the side.

Enjoy preparing and savoring these delicious Japanese dishes!

Miso-marinated Fish

Ingredients:

- 2 pieces of white fish (e.g., cod, salmon)
- 1/4 cup miso paste (white or red)
- 2 tbsp sake
- 1 tbsp mirin
- 1 tbsp sugar

Instructions:

1. **Make Marinade:** In a bowl, mix miso paste, sake, mirin, and sugar until smooth.
2. **Marinate Fish:** Coat the fish with the marinade and refrigerate for at least 30 minutes (up to overnight).
3. **Cook:** Preheat the oven to 400°F (200°C). Remove excess marinade and bake fish for about 15-20 minutes until cooked through.
4. **Serve:** Serve with rice and pickled vegetables.

Tofu Steak

Ingredients:

- 1 block firm tofu, drained
- 2 tbsp soy sauce
- 1 tbsp sesame oil
- 1 tbsp green onions, chopped
- Optional: sliced mushrooms or other vegetables

Instructions:

1. **Prepare Tofu:** Cut the tofu into thick slices and press to remove excess moisture.
2. **Marinate:** In a bowl, mix soy sauce and sesame oil. Marinate tofu for about 15 minutes.
3. **Cook:** Heat a pan over medium heat. Sauté tofu until golden brown on both sides, about 4-5 minutes per side.
4. **Serve:** Top with green onions and serve with rice.

Tsukemono (Pickled Vegetables)

Ingredients:

- 1 cucumber, sliced
- 1 carrot, julienned
- 1 daikon radish, sliced
- 1/4 cup rice vinegar
- 2 tbsp sugar
- 1 tsp salt
- Optional: chili flakes for heat

Instructions:

1. **Prepare Vegetables:** Combine sliced cucumber, carrot, and daikon in a bowl.
2. **Make Pickling Solution:** In a separate bowl, mix rice vinegar, sugar, salt, and chili flakes.
3. **Pickle:** Pour the pickling solution over the vegetables and let sit for at least 30 minutes.
4. **Serve:** Serve chilled or at room temperature.

Yaki Soba (Fried Noodles)

Ingredients:

- 8 oz yakisoba noodles (or ramen noodles)
- 1 cup cabbage, chopped
- 1 carrot, julienned
- 1 bell pepper, sliced
- 1/4 cup soy sauce
- 2 tbsp Worcestershire sauce
- 1 tbsp sesame oil
- Optional: protein (chicken, pork, shrimp)

Instructions:

1. **Cook Noodles:** Boil noodles according to package instructions. Drain and set aside.
2. **Stir-fry Vegetables:** In a large pan, heat sesame oil over medium heat. Add vegetables and protein, cooking until tender.
3. **Add Noodles:** Stir in the cooked noodles, soy sauce, and Worcestershire sauce. Toss to combine and heat through.
4. **Serve:** Serve hot, garnished with pickled ginger or green onions if desired.

Chashu Pork

Ingredients:

- 1 lb pork belly
- 1/4 cup soy sauce
- 1/4 cup mirin
- 1/4 cup sake
- 1 tbsp sugar
- 2 green onions, chopped
- Ginger slices

Instructions:

1. **Prepare Pork:** Roll the pork belly tightly and tie with kitchen twine.
2. **Sear Pork:** In a pot, sear the pork belly on all sides until browned.
3. **Add Sauce:** Add soy sauce, mirin, sake, sugar, green onions, and ginger. Cover and simmer for 1-2 hours until tender.
4. **Slice and Serve:** Let cool, then slice thinly. Serve over rice or in ramen.

Goya Champuru (Bitter Melon Stir-fry)

Ingredients:

- 1 bitter melon, sliced
- 1 block tofu, cubed
- 1/2 lb pork (or other protein), sliced
- 2 tbsp soy sauce
- 1 tbsp sesame oil
- 1 clove garlic, minced

Instructions:

1. **Sauté Tofu:** In a pan, heat sesame oil and fry the tofu cubes until golden. Remove and set aside.
2. **Cook Pork:** In the same pan, sauté the pork until cooked through.
3. **Add Vegetables:** Add bitter melon and garlic, cooking until the melon is tender.
4. **Combine:** Return tofu to the pan and stir in soy sauce. Cook for another 2-3 minutes.
5. **Serve:** Serve hot over rice.

Yudofu (Hot Tofu)

Ingredients:

- 1 block silken tofu
- 4 cups dashi broth
- Soy sauce (for dipping)
- Chopped green onions and grated ginger (for garnish)

Instructions:

1. **Heat Broth:** In a pot, bring dashi broth to a gentle simmer.
2. **Add Tofu:** Carefully add the block of tofu and simmer for about 5 minutes until heated through.
3. **Serve:** Serve the tofu in bowls with dipping soy sauce and garnish with green onions and ginger.

Shio Ramen (Salt Ramen)

Ingredients:

- 4 cups chicken or pork broth
- 2 servings ramen noodles
- 1 tbsp soy sauce
- 1 tsp salt
- Toppings: sliced chashu pork, green onions, boiled egg, nori, and bamboo shoots

Instructions:

1. **Prepare Broth:** In a pot, heat the broth with soy sauce and salt.
2. **Cook Noodles:** Boil ramen noodles according to package instructions. Drain and set aside.
3. **Assemble Bowls:** In serving bowls, add noodles, then ladle hot broth over them.
4. **Top:** Add desired toppings and serve hot.

Gyudon (Beef Bowl)

Ingredients:

- 1 lb thinly sliced beef
- 1 onion, sliced
- 1/4 cup soy sauce
- 1/4 cup mirin
- 2 tbsp sugar
- 2 cups cooked rice
- Sliced green onions (for garnish)
- Pickled ginger (for serving)

Instructions:

1. **Cook Onions:** In a pan, sauté onions until translucent.
2. **Add Beef:** Add sliced beef and cook until browned.
3. **Season:** Stir in soy sauce, mirin, and sugar. Simmer for about 5 minutes.
4. **Serve:** Serve beef mixture over rice, garnished with green onions and pickled ginger.

Enjoy creating and savoring these delicious Japanese dishes!

www.ingramcontent.com/pod-product-compliance
Lightning Source LLC
LaVergne TN
LVHW081340060526
838201LV00055B/2762